East Anglian Book of Verse

CONTENTS

DEDICATION

I dedicate these verses to all my East Anglian friends who supported my first venture into print so generously and thus made this second volume possible. Thank you!

Mary Wise

6\9\91

DOWN BY THE RIVER AT ELY.

There are launches and Cruisers
And house-boats on view
Down by the River at Ely,
There are long-boats & barges
And narrow boats too
Down by the River at Ely.
There are ducks by the score
And moorhens galore
Down by the River at Ely.
Swans glide into view
There are Chinese geese too
Down by the River at Ely.
Smart Rowing Eights meet
Their rivals to greet
Down by the River at Ely.
An Old Bridge is seen
Adding grace to the scene
Down by the River at Ely.
Willows enhance the stream
Grass grows emerald green
Down by the River at Ely
And the Maltings stand tall
Approving it all
Down by the River at Ely.
There are folk walking dogs,
Joggers in running togs
Down by the River at Ely
There are folk taking snaps
Children feeding ducks scraps
Down by the River at Ely
People find time to stare
At the loveliness there
Down by the River at Ely
So why not take pleasure
By spending some leisure
Down by the River at Ely?

MEMORIES OF A LIFETIME.

Navy serge gym-slip, black stockings, striped tie,
Panama hats and hair ribbons awry,
Angela Brazil, a Classic or two,
School days I remember with pleasure, do you?

Macclesfield silk and Henry Heath Hats,
Crocodile shoes and gents in fawn spats,
"The Maid of the Mountains" "The Desert Song" too
These teenage memories I cherish do you?

We hobbled in Hobble skirts,
Slouched in Cloche hats,
Laughed at the antics of Felix the Cat,
Pip, Squeak and Wilfred were prime favourites too,
These things I remember with pleasure, do you?

The first Talking Pictures, The Charleston, long beads,
Short skimpy skirts that showed off our knees.
The Bob and the Shingle, the Eaton crop too
All these I remember with pleasure, do you?

Ethel M. Dell, P.G. Wodehouse, Zane Gray
All these were avidly read in my day
We flocked to the Movies to see Sonny Boy,
The Jazz Singer too gave spontaneous joy,
Our Make-up was simple. Nail Varnish was new.
All this I remember with pleasure, do you?

Postal deliveries three times a day,
Telegram Boys cycled smartly away,
Steam-Trains and Stations
Kept tidy and bright.
Coal fires in waiting rooms
Blazed through the night,
We hadn't much cash but we found lots to do
These are the things I remember, do you?

2

Some people were lucky, there were 'Haves' and "Havenots"
Riches and Poverty,
Limousines and Pawn Shops
Bright Young Things sparkled
While Champagne corks popped
Amy Johnson flew Solo and conquered the Blue
These are the things I remember, do you?

Then came the War Years
The Partings the tears,
Shelters and "Doodle-bugs" black-outs and fears,
Clothing Coupons, fire-watching and Evacuees,
Sufficient to feed us but no luxuries.
Digging for Victory, Overtime too
These are the things I remember, do you?

Spam, Powdered eggs, and Whalemeat. Oh dear!
Most things were rationed, there wasn't much beer.
Churchill inspired us, Tommy Handley amused,
Vera Lynn touched our hearts, while our Allies enthused.
Friendship upheld us, with nothing to spare
Everyone eager and willing to share.
The end of Hostilities, Life starting anew.
All this I remember, and gratefully too!

THE FORTY FOOT.

Man-made and straight the Forty Foot runs slow
But on it's Banks King Cup and Bulrush grow,
And in the stillness of the early morn
A Heron's cry upon the breeze is borne.
Here haughty Swan and impish Moorhen glide
And leave a gentle tell-tale wake behind.
On Waterlily raft a shy Vole gnaws

A dainty morsel held between it's paws,
Sleek Rats ascurry in the whistling reeds
Startle a timid Duckling as he feeds.
Perchance, when Moonlight penetrates his holt,
A velvet Otter makes a sudden bolt,
Whilst snowy Barn Owl solemnly surveys
Musing on Nature's enigmatic ways.

Within the Waters Roach and Bream abound
To make an Anglers' happy hunting ground
From near and far in friendly silence they
With trembling line await their silver prey,
Forgetful of all else, come sun or rain
They cast aside the weight of workday strain.

When hoary Winter's frozen fingers grasp
The Forty Foot within an icy clasp
The rosy Skaters, timorous or bold,
Enhance the scene with scarlet, blue and gold,
Impatient e'er the fitful Sunlight fades
To etch the surface with their steely blades.

On either Bank the flat, black acres lie
stretching uninterupted to the sky
Giving a fair return for arduous toil
To those who wrest a living from the soil.
A Blessing on Cornelius Vermuyden
Who cut this Dyke to drain the Fertile Fen
And left an all enduring legacy
Bequeathing Beauty, Sport and Industry.

NORFOLK.

Norfolk is a forthright County
Famous in so many ways,
With a "down to earth" reaction
Where a man means what he says.
Bears an honest reputation
Looks life squarely in the face,
Norfolk folk are always willing
They are such a special race.

Many famous Sons has Norfolk,
And famous daughters not a few,
Nelson was born at Burnham
Charles Dickens well Gt. Yarmouth knew,
Clarkson, Windham, and George Borrow
All originated here,
Norfolk Men who from the pages
Of History ne'er will disappear.
Boadicea, Edith Cavell, Annie Lubbock,
Lizzie Fry
Just a few East Anglian ladies
Whose endeavours will not die.

All the Royals cherish Norfolk
And the freedom that it brings.
Sandringham in wooded splendour
The beloved home of Kings.
Norfolk where the pheasant prospers
And erotic Wildlife range,
The most English, English County
Please God it may never change.

EVOLUTION.

The Garden of Eden, they tell us
Beheld the creation of Man,
Adam tasted the apple
But refused to "carry the can".

"It's none of my doing," he told them,
Or so we are led to believe.
He just wouldn't shoulder the onus,
But planted it firmly on Eve!

Then Darwin declared that Gorillas
Were the true antecedents of Man
"The Origin of the Species" he called it,
And avidly worked on that plan.

The Scientists vowed a bit later
That something crawled out of a bog
And that was in fact Man's beginning
(They entered it all in a log)

Now Astronomers say that the "Big Bang"
Caused all the Planets to dance
And from then on Evolution
Was merely a matter of chance.

Everyone seeks the solution
To Life's great enigma it seems
But surely chance isn't the answer
There must be a definite scheme

Could chance form the tail of a peacock?
Could chance paint a butterfly's wing
Could chance fashion delicate blossom
Or inspire a blackbird to sing?

Though accident may be the reason
That triggers off most of Man's strife
There must be divine motivation,
Chance can't be the answer to Life.'

MARCH ANCIENT AND MODERN.

A busy little Fenland town is March
That's growing all the time,
You see houses in the evening
That weren't there at breakfast-time!
The Shops are bright and cheerful,
There's a Market twice a week
When Britannia on the old Town Hall
Awakens from her sleep.
The River Nene flows slowly on
Whilst traffic tries to speed along.
There's an Auction every Wednesday
Held in the Palace Hall
Where you can bid for anything
However large or small.
The "Mayor" in 1988
Is Mrs. Patsy Brewin,
A lady who without a doubt
Is always "up and doing"
Most Public spirited is she
And busy as a hiving bee.
She'll have a 'go' at anything
That honour to March town will bring,
And though her Mayoral Gown won't fit
Methinks she very well fills it!
St Wendreda's Church stands proud and tall
It's steeple 140 ft. overall.
Carved Angels grace the inner roof
As Dorothy Sayers gives proof
In her "Nine Taylors", they do tell
Miss Sayers knew March town quite well.
In busy Broad St. shoppers throng
And round the Fountain hurry on,
Few glancing this Victorian shrine
Although it's really rather fine.

March once a thriving Railway town
With famous Marshalling Yard
Europe's largest so they say
Alas no longer so to-day.
Soon March will host a Prison Block
(It's being built at Whitemoor)
So peace should flourish even more
With retribution at it's door!
This ancient little Fenland town
Dates back to Saxon times.
T'was known as Merchford in those days
And though it's changed in myraid ways
Its Sons still boast a touch of "starch"
That typified those Men of March.

THE SISTERS (SUCCESS AND FAILURE)

SUCCESS.

Fair she is as almond blossom,
Lovely as a laughing bride,
Widely sought and richly feted,
Courtiers on every side.

Fickle as an April morning
Here a frown and there a smile
Men do battle for her favours
But to find her gone meanwhile.

Few can claim that she has lingered,
Many know her swift caress.
She is but a man made godess,
This much coverted Success.

FAILURE.

Dark she is as Elderberry
Sober as a Quaker maid
Coldly met and curtly greeted
Seldom hears a tribute paid.

Welcome as a bleak North Easter,
Dour of manner, dull of eye
Men but glance in her direction
In their urge to hurry by.

Some she leads on to destruction
Others she lifts up to Fame
Who shall say he has not met her
Failure is her dreary name.

Yet sometimes when mischief beckons
Sister may fill sister's role,
Leaving riddles for the future
To decipher on Life's scroll.

"WHISTLING JIM" Pilot Officer J.W. Hocking

So young yet so resourceful,
So fearless and so brave,
A young Australian Pilot
Gave all, March town to save.
Just twenty one in nineteen forty four
He didn't hesitate to act,
Although he knew the "score".
So when the Stirling 'plane he flew
Was doomed, his duty swiftly knew,
And as it took it's fatal dive
He told his crew to look alive
"Go on lads, hurry, out you go.
This is the only way I know!"
So in a field close to st. Wendreda's Church
The stricken aircraft crashed upon the earth
It's noble pilot knowing well the cost
Gave his young life so others were not lost.
Now a Memorial upon an ancient wall
Within St. Wendreda's Church recalls it all
While Hocking Court will keep this memory green
Whenever his illustrious name is seen.
And so the gratitude of March will never fade
Remembering Jim Hocking
And the sacrifice he made!

8

NO FRIEND OF MINE.

He is no friend of mine
Who fells a tree
That from the heat of Summer
Shelters me.
That bears exotic blossom in the Spring,
Whose gold in Autumn
Is a wondrous thing.
He is no friend of mine
Who fells a tree.
He loves not Nature so how
Could he be?

He is no friend of mine
Who fells a tree
That paints a Winter wonderland for me
A living landmark I have loved and known
And 'neath whose sturdy branches I have grown
He is no friend of mine
Who fells a tree.
He loves not nature
So how could he be?

He is no friend of mine
Who fells a tree
That is a sanctuary for Bird and bee,
Within whose shadow mouse and squirrel play
And Children find a happy hideaway
He is no friend of mine
Who fells a tree
He loves not Nature so how could he be?

NEWMARKET.

There's a special atmosphere about Newmarket
Where special kinds of people walk about,
There's a lot of Harris tweed and real leather
In shop windows horsey gear is paramount.

Every little chap one meets could be a jockey,
Grown men no bigger than a teenage lad,
There are horsey looking ladies in the High Street,
And a few eccentrics looking slightly mad.

There are Stable boys in high-necked yellow sweaters,
And riding boots that seem a trifle big,
There are Grooms with prematurely wrinkled faces
And Stable Girls in multi-coloured rig.

There are signs that tell you to "Beware of Horses"
And on the Heath fantastic horsemen trot.
There are Race Days when you can't get near the centre
And queues prevent you getting to the shops.

And then, of course, when Tattershall's in session
You well may see the noble and the grand
Yes Newmarket is very stimulating
One of the finest Towns that grace our land.

FRIENDS

Friends come in all shapes and sizes,
Depths and thickness too.
Some are always loyal
And some make use of you.
Some you can rely on
No matter what fate may bring
You know they will stand beside you
To lessen life's sharp sting,
Some love you for yourself alone,
(Thin on the ground this kind)
Others fawn upon you with benefit in mind.
Fair-weather friends are missing
Whene'er the going's tough.
When the road's smooth they're with you,
But have "other plans" when rough.
In just a few you can confide.
From most your secrets you must hide.
Some friends elate you, some deflate
While others just exasperate,
Some friends delight, some you'll find tight,
While one or two just fade from sight.
So many and so varied, now please don't get me wrong,
I love them all but my Best Friend
Is the one who holds her tongue!

MOTHER.

She makes no claim
To brilliance or renown
Nor does sophistication
Make her frown
She is content to fill
The niche she's made
And face each day's
Upheavals unafraid.

She takes delight
In many simple things.
That dewy freshness
That the morning brings,
A child's laugh
A sprig of mignonette,
A sparrow's gratitude,
A Kitchenette.

She makes no claim
To beauty but her eyes
Are soft and kind
And infinitely wise,
Her joy she finds
In giving to another,
Her name most beautiful
of all - is MOTHER.

THE VISION

I saw a nation rise from out the fire
A Nation purged of greed and self desire
With Unity upon her banners writ
And all her people by one purpose knit.

I saw a mighty Citadel arise
With gleaming turrets towering to the skies
And with a gate so wondrous high and wide
That all who wished might quickly pass inside.

I saw new Cities planned and built by youth
Upon the sure foundation stone of truth
I found a fiery zest that only war
Had ever wakened in our breasts before.

I saw a generation free and strong
With will to strive and time to right the wrong
I saw Art reinstated on her throne
And honest effort come into it's own.

I saw false gods abandoned for the true
Old values cast aside in place of new
I saw the aged cared for and content
And energies on worthwhile purpose spent.

I saw the Demon Want at last cast out
And watched the death of misbelief and doubt
I saw a land, if not for heros, then
A land at least befitting Englishmen.

"SHAW'S CORNER." AYOT ST LAWRENCE.

Down winding lanes
Through Hawthorn scented byways
With bluebells carpeting the wayside woods
We came at last to that secluded haven
Where GBS spent his declining days.

An unpretentious home
Where peace abided
Where he would write sometimes, sometimes relax
And where still lingered that undaunted presence
No literary demand could overtax.

His Hats still hang on that old fashioned Hallstand
Deer-stalker, Panama, Beekeeper's Veil
His favourite Homburg too in prime condition
Despite the passing of some 60 years.
And close beside his Walking sticks and gaiters
One almost sees his tall, gaunt figure stalk
His shoes still standing
Waiting at the ready
For him to take his customary walk

His Study too remains as he last left it
Equipped with all the things a writer needs
Pens. Reference and Filing Cabinets
Typewriter for Miss Patch to use at speed
Upon the walls his friends look down upon him
Wicksteed and Morris, Chesterton and Yates
Gene Tunney too and J.M Barrie
To mention just a few, all all-time greats.

The Drawing-room is dignified yet cosy,
In the Dining-room his "treasures" come to light,
His favourite pocket-watch and gold propelling pencil,
The Wireless Set he listened to each night.

The Spartan kitchen Mrs. Laden's sanctum,
Scrupulously clean, as it had been in use
And well equipped with necessary gadgets
Those tasty, meatless dishes to produce.

The house is set in an enchanting garden
With velvet lawns and tall exotic trees,
A stately Elm, Yew, Copper Beech and Cedar,
A Mulberry bush all glorify the view,

And tucked away in solitary seclusion
Where it would catch the Sun's last dying rays,
The Writer's "Hut" still stands to mark the birthplace
Of those enthralling and immortal Plays.

DOCTOR MEADOWS.

We had an old Physician
Doctor Meadows was his name
And when anyone was poorly
He to our rescue came.
No DHSS in those days,
In case we might be ill
My Mother kept a special fund
So she could pay his bill

I loved this gentle healer
Though I knew he was too wise
To let a little girl of six
Pull wool over his eyes
Once when School palled a little
I faked a nasty chill
But wily Doctor Meadows
Knew I wasn't really ill
"All right" he said "Let's hear you cough"
And when I did he told me off!

The Family feared I had gone mad
When I started to write verse
But dear old Doctor Meadows said
"Ah well it could be worse
Just let her have her head a bit
And hope that she grows out of it!"

When I was seventeen alas
I had to have an Op
Nothing very serious
But I liked it not a lot
"Do you think I'm going to die?" I asked
He gave a little smile
"Not you!" he said for goodness sake
You've got a lot more Hearts to break!"

"INN" FORMATION WANTED!

How many "Locals" in Chatteris?
You can count them on one hand to-day
But an old fellow told me in High Street
There were scores in his Grandfather's day
He remembered the Boar's Head and Anchor,
The Woolpack, the Fen Plough and Ship,
The Cricketers' Arms, Horse & Jockey,
Where resounded many a quip.
King William the 4th. and the Wheatsheaf,
The Greyhound, the Cross Keys and Crown,
The Brickmakers' Arms and the Five Bells,
All these Inns once flourished in town.
Silver Jubilee, White Hart & Blue Ball,
The George, Spade & Becket and Cock,
Golden Lion, Railway Tavern & Three Pots,
All answered the Traveller's knock.
The Grenadiers, Black Horse & Boat House,
Five Horseshoes. Red Lion and Hoops,
Lamb & Flag, Boot & Slipper, White Lion,
Where Fenmen were happy to troop.
The Prince of Wales Feathers, the New Hoops,
Hare & Hounds and the Golden Drop too,
Farmer's Boy, Elephant & Castle
All these had a welcome for you
Must be others that haven't been mentioned
Can you recall their names?
So they are never forgotten
As long as a memory remains.

ASPIRATIONS

To live each day as though you were immortal
No fear of lurking death or dread decay
To work as though your energies were boundless
And think not of tomorrow but to-day.

To have no dread of that uncertain future
That oft times clouds the present with it's threat
To make the most of each and every dawning
And crown it with the greatest effort yet.

To have no doubt achievement is rewarding
No matter if applause be faint or strong
To keep your ideals when your faith is shaken
And have the courage to oppose the wrong.

To make allowance for another's weakness
Yet sternly crush when in yourself 'tis rife
To do all this is to fulfil your mission
And so obtain the very best from life

MAYOR'S NEST.

Miss Selyam-Barking
Got had up for parking
Her Mini outside the Town Hall
An Official said "Madam
This sacred McAdam
Is reserved for the Mayor
And that's all."

Said Miss Selyam-Barking
"You must Sir be larking
I'm not moving from here and that's that
The reason for why,
If you've got half an eye
Is because all my tyres are flat!

Miss Selyam-Barking
Got had up for Parking
But she didn't care not one cuss
She did all her shopping
And went home to Wapping
On a New Corporation Bus!

WAYWARD WOMAN!!

Man is complex
Woman's worse
For she has the
Double curse
Of a heart
As soft as soap
And a temper
Rough as rope.

Please her
And she'll give
Her all.
Anything that's on her stall
Irritate her
And beware
Behold a tiger
In a snare.

Man is complex
So they say
But not in a
Woman's way.
She is sweet
And true and kind
Only if she has
The mind!

Treat her then
With double care
Even though she
Be at prayer
For beneath
That creamy skin
You may find
A Witch within.

HRH PRINCESS BEATRICE ELIZABETH MARY.

Here's to a Daughter of the House of York
Delivered proudly by a Royal Stork
Upon a unique and auspicious date
The Eighth day of the Eighth Month '88
At eighteen minutes past eight precisely,
Methinks she got that worked out very nicely!

So here's a toast unto our new Princess
May love surround her in a warm caress
Give her some beauty and a lot of brain
That she specific knowledge may obtain
God grant her Happiness but most of all
The Spirit to endure whate'er befall!

GREAT YARMOUTH   1920

"Yarmouth"
And instantly
The tangled years
Lie in a tidy coil
Within my reach
For I am young again.

Upon the Jetty
Old Salts sit and spin
Their gaudy yarns
Broidered by fancy's silk
Whilst childrens laughter
On the crowded beach
Mingles with Punch's
Well beloved screech.

Behind the Promenade
Straggles the ancient town
With close built rows
That grope down to the Quay
Where, when the Summer Steamers
Are laid by
The Drifters strain
Impatient for the sea

And on the Wharf
Where Gaelic vies with drawl
And sequinned herring
Catch the fretful sun
The burly skippers
Stand morosely by
To watch the Salesmen
With a wary eye.

Then Highland Lassies
Gut the shimmering fish
With wonderous speed
And when 'tis done
Search the shop windows
Knitting as they roam
To find a 'giftie'
For the bairns at home.

But it is Winter
That I best recall
When high seas crash
Headlong against the pier
When the last visitor
Has said "Goodbye"
And nought is left
But Sand and Sea and Sky.

"Yarmouth"
And instantly
Memory's swift tide
Sweeps back
Forgotten scenes
And I am young again.

MEMORY.

A Magical Carpet of countless cross threads
With curious patterns engraved
Mysterious shapings and patches of shade
Drab corners with flowers interplaced.
Each day has some colour to add to the scheme
Each mood leaves indelible sign,
And each human contact, no matter how small,
Has an ultimate place in design.

A book of queer fragments,
Of songs and of verse,
Each with a label attached.
Scraps of philosophy, proverbs galore
And sayings on childhood's slate scratched.
A Visitors' Book, signed by friend and by foe
Sometimes even marked with a cross.
A Record that stands with no entry defaced
And nothing omitted or lost.

A carved treasure chest that is full to the brim
With trinkets and jewels and trash,
Precious silk rubbing sides with the roughest of serge
And tapestry mounted on crash.
Portrait and minature, landscape and view
Oftimes made misty by tears,
Fragments of granite and oddments of jade
Rediscovered again through the years!

MISCELLANEOUS THOUGHTS.

SLEEP.

The Brain's a Computer
That works on Life's screen
And sleep is the button
That wipes it all clean.

****

OPPORTUNITY.

"Opportunity knocks but once"
So some folk say,
But watch this most elusive maid
As she pursues her way
And you will see she seldom knocks
Or makes the slightest din
The wise are waiting at the door
To drag the Lady in!

****

CONTENTMENT.

Grumbling about my lot
And all the things I hadn't got
A Happy man said "Give to me
Neither Wealth nor Poverty!"

TO THE FUTURE!

We pause in 1988 our efforts to expostulate,
We've split the atom, reached the moon,
Found Oil at Sea, made business boom,
Seen Heart transplants, and Test-tube Babes,
Hip joints replaced, Ladies "re-faced."
Watched Students change before our eyes,
Scholars become computerised.
What marvels will the future hold
And our descendants see unfold?
A Robot that can work and talk
Then take the Poodle for a walk.
A tool that can put back the clocks
So one may re-live Life's bright spots,
A Method to control the rain
So outdoor "Do's" are not in vain.
Time stored away for when one needs it.
A Garden weedless once you seed it.
A Car that can move sideways too
Requires no juice and folds in two,
A magnet key the lock that finds
A Wedding ring that really binds,
A gland that does in truth renew
And makes man live a thou' or two.
A preparation for the fair
A pleasant drink that tints the hair
A tunnel all the world around
An instrument so things are found.
A trip to Mars for 50p
All this may in the future be!

TOMORROW.

How wise the Providence that blinds our eyes
To future days with thoughts and acts unknown
For should we mount the rocky paths ahead
If we could see our courses plainly shown?

What wisdom. That contrived tomorrow's mist
That man might hope and hoping live to-day
In unknown regions do we build out dreams
To-day is sad, tomorrow who shall say?

NORFOLK DELIGHTS

A Jacket for the gentleman;
Sweet lavender for missus,
Turkeys at Christmas time,
Ducklings and other dishes,
And then, of course, there's Ploughman's lunch
Washed down by lots of Norfolk Punch.

A Banquet for the epicure,
Lobsters and crabs from Cromer,
Plump Yarmouth bloaters in a pan,
Norfolk dumplings boiling over.
Cockles from Moorston round and fat,
Mussels from Wells black as your hat.
You must appreciate all these
Unless you're very hard to please.

TONGUE-TIED.

When I try to say what's on my mind
Words fail me;
Convey my feelings to Mankind
Words fail me
All I can do is touch a hand
And hope my friend will understand
I have no speech at my command
Words fail me!

When I struggle to express a thought
Words fail me
All my striving comes to nought
Words fail me
And so I fall back on my pen
And everything is simple then
I make myself explicit when
Words fail me!

CATS.

Lots of Pussies in the past we've had
And swore each was the last,
But it never came to that,
For Life we found without a Cat
Is very, very, very Flat!

These wilful creatures rule our lives
Dumb Animals? Gods in disguise!
They gaze at us with doting eyes
Beware they're very, very wise.

Cats are curious, full of fun,
Love to frolic in the sun,
Careful, for those velvet paws
Hide very, very cruel claws.

Nothing beguiles quite like a cat
It's "Home" when one sits on the mat.
Yes though sometimes they can be teasing,
CATS are very, very, pleasing.

TIT FOR TAT.

When George and 1 were married
My dear Aunt Fanny said
"I wonder if you realise young man
Just what you've wed
I wish you every happiness,
I'm sure that is your due
But you've got a few surprises
Winging their way to you!"

This didn't please me very much,
She was my favourite Aunt,
So I gave her a little nudge
And looked at her askant
Fair comment! well it could so be
But what she didn't say
Was that I had a few sharp shocks
About to come by way!

MASTERPIECE.

This painting executed with such skill
That hangs on the rocky wall of fate
Uncouth and ugly if one gazes close
Judged from afar it's beauties fascinate.

No thoughtless daub with colours careless picked
Each shade is blended by a master hand
And though sometimes to our untutored eye
The Colours clash, we learn to understand.

Youth cries "Tis hard, a softer tone were best"
Whereas experience knows contrast's worth
The Artist's vision sees the scene complete
Before his brilliant pencil gives it birth.

Take heart then Model, patient take your stand,
The finished canvas is alone the test
Unless you know the glories of his brush
How can you say which colour scheme is best?

BEGINNERS PLEASE!

ALL THESE PERSONALITIES
DIED IN 1984

"We'll stage a Play" St Peter said
"In Nineteen Eighty Four, A noble Play,
The like of which has not been seen before.
Let J.B. Priestley write the Script.
John Betjeman the Verse, and Reggie Bosanquet can prompt
Whene'er the Cast rehearse.
Let gentle Tommy Cooper his fumbling Magic show.
And Eric Morecambe's Comedy with effervescence flow.
Let Flora Robson's dignity reflect her studied Art
And Down-to earth Diana Dors with courage play her part.
Let genial James Mason add glamour to the scene
And bardic Richard Burton clinch a Producer's dream.
"We'll stage a Play" St Peter said
In Nineteen Eighty Four
A noble Play the like of which
Has not been seen before.
No sacrifice shall be in vain, Earth's loss is truly
Heaven's Gain!"